Country Fil
Great Britain

Clare Oliver

FRANKLIN WATTS
LONDON•SYDNEY

Revised and updated 2006

Franklin Watts
338 Euston Road, London
NW1 3BH

Franklin Watts Australia
Hachette Children's Books
Level 17/207 Kent Street
Sydney NSW 2000

COUNTRY FILE: GREAT BRITAIN produced for Franklin Watts
by Bender Richardson White, PO Box 266, Uxbridge, UK.
Project Editor: Lionel Bender
Text Editor: Peter Harrison
Designer: Ben White
Picture Researcher: Cathy Stastny
Media Conversion and Make-up: Mike Pilley, Radius
Production: Kim Richardson

Graphics: Mike Pilley, Radius
Maps: Stefan Chabluk

For Franklin Watts:
Series Editor: Adrian Cole
Art Director: Jonathan Hair

A CIP catalogue record for this book is available
from the British Library.

ISBN 0 7496 6638 2

Dewey Classification: 914.1

Printed in China

Picture Credits

Pages: 1: PhotoDisc Inc./Jeremy Hoare. 3: PhotoDisc
Inc./Andrew Ward/Life File. 4: PhotoDisc Inc/Colin
Paterson. 6: Hutchison Photo Library/Robert Francis.
8: Hutchison Photo Library/Jeremy Horner.
9: Hutchison Photo Library/Peter Morzynski. 10 top:
PhotoDisc Inc./Andrew Ward/Life File. 10–11 bottom:
PhotoDisc Inc./Jeremy Hoare. 12 DAS Photo/David
Simson. 14–15 bottom: Hutchison Photo Library.
16–17: Eye Ubiquitous/G. Daniels. 18 top: John
Walmsley Photography. 18 bottom: Ted Spiegal/Corbis
Images. 20: Hutchison Photo Library/Bernard Gérard.
21: Eye Ubiquitous/Martin Foyle. 22: Hutchison Photo
Library/Bernard Gérard. 23: PhotoDisc Inc./Andrew
Ward/Life File. 24: Peter Tumley/Corbis Images. 26
PhotoDisc Inc./Andrew Ward/Life File. 28: Reuters
NewMedia Inc./Corbis Images. 29: Howard Davis/Corbis
Images. 30: PhotoDisc Inc./John Wang. 31: PhotoDisc
Inc./Andrew Ward/Life File.
Cover photo: James Davis Travel Photography.

Note to parents and teachers

Every effort has been made by the Publishers to ensure
that the websites in this book are suitable for children,
that they are of the highest educational value, and that
they contain no inappropriate or offensive material.
However, because of the nature of the Internet, it is
impossible to guarantee that the contents of these sites
will not be altered. We strongly advise that Internet
access is supervised by a responsible adult.

The Author

Clare Oliver is a full-time writer and
editor of non-fiction books. She has
written more than 50 books for children.
This is her second book about Great
Britain.

Contents

Welcome to Great Britain

Great Britain is made up of the kingdoms of England and Scotland and the principality of Wales. Together with the province of Northern Ireland, it is part of the United Kingdom (UK). The UK is a member of the European Union (EU).

The mainland of Great Britain is one of the two largest islands to the west of continental Europe. The other island is Ireland, where the British province of Northern Ireland is situated. Several island groups and thousands of smaller islands are also part of Great Britain.

Worldwide influence

Great Britain is famous as the birthplace of the Industrial Revolution. It was the first nation in the world to shift from an economy based on agriculture to one based on industry and manufacturing. Despite its small land area, Great Britain controlled a large colonial empire until the early 20th century. It still plays a key role in global events. The nation's principal language, English, is now a world language of business and culture.

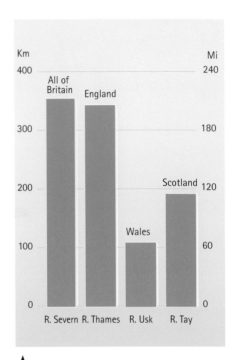

The length of Britain's longest rivers. The River Severn runs through England and Wales and is the longest overall.

Eilean Donan Castle in the Scottish Highlands has been a fortified site for 800 years. The present castle dates from the early 20th century. ▼

The Land

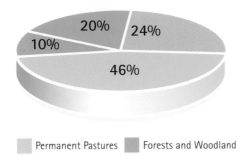

Permanent Pastures — Forests and Woodland
Other — Arable Land

▲▲ Land use in Great Britain.

A rural landscape in southern England – rolling hills, fields, hedges, trees and a country house. ▼▼

The British landscape varies from green, rolling hills to steep mountains. A mild, wet climate keeps much of the land fertile.

The wettest places are mountainous western regions, such as the Highlands of northern Scotland, the Lake District in north-west England and Snowdonia in north Wales. These all receive more than 3,000 millimetres of rain each year. The east is much drier, and some places there average less than 700 millimetres of rain a year.

The Highlands include Britain's highest peak, Ben Nevis (1,343 metres). Deep lakes, called lochs, fill the Highland valleys. The central part of Scotland, called the Central Lowlands, consists of low, rolling hills. Watered by the rivers Clyde, Forth and Tay, this region is mostly farmland.

A varied landscape and climate

Towards the border with England, the land rises again, first with the Southern Upland range, and then the Cheviot Hills. Northern England is rugged and bleak and includes Cumbria's mountainous Lake District. The region features England's highest peak, Scafell Pike (978 metres).

The Pennines are a chain of hills that run like a spine from northern England to the Midlands. Here, the Rivers Severn, Trent and Avon have formed valleys. Central and eastern England are mostly made up of low plains. There are chalk hills called downs in the south, and rugged moors and rocky coasts to the south-west.

The Welsh landscape includes, in the north, Britain's second-highest peak, Mount Snowdon (1,085 metres), and in the south, the mountainous Brecon Beacons.

The average annual temperature in Great Britain ranges from about 7 °C on the north-easterly island of Shetland, to about 11 °C on the Cornish coast in the south-west.

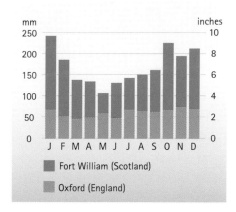

Fort William (Scotland)

Oxford (England)

 Annual rainfall comparison between towns in Scotland and England.

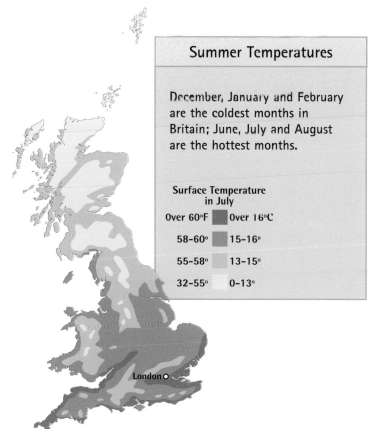

Summer Temperatures

December, January and February are the coldest months in Britain; June, July and August are the hottest months.

Surface Temperature
in July

Over 60°F		Over 16°C
58-60°		15-16°
55-58°		13-15°
32-55°		0-13°

London○

Animal Life

Great Britain's mammals include deer, squirrels, a species of mole, badgers, foxes and rabbits, hares, mice and bats.

Among reptiles and amphibians are lizards, frogs, newts and toads, but snakes are unknown in most places except the south and south-east.

Birdlife includes several types of gulls, ducks, geese, tits and swans as well as ptarmigan, golden eagles and grey herons.

Web Search ▶▶

▶ www.met-office.gov.uk
World and British weather information from the Meteorological Office.

7

The People

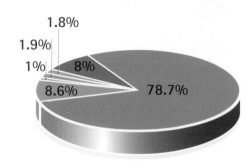

English   Scottish   Irish   Welsh
Ulster   West Indian, Indian, Pakistani and Others

1.8%
1.9%
1%
8%
8.6%
78.7%

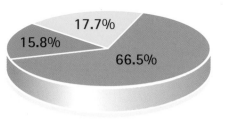

▲
▲ The percentage of ethnic groups that make up the British people.

D espite its small land area, Britain is home to over 60 million people. As well as the native Scots, Welsh and English, many other ethnic groups have settled in Britain over the centuries.

Scottish people account for nearly 10 per cent of the population. Less than 2 per cent of the population are Welsh. The Scots and Welsh are descendants of the Celts, who settled the islands in prehistoric times. The English, who make up 82 per cent of the population, take their name from the Angles, a Germanic tribe that arrived in the 5th and 6th centuries AD.

After World War II, people from former British colonies such as India, Hong Kong and the West Indies were encouraged to come to Britain to help re-establish the workforce. People from immigrant ethnic groups now account for nearly 8 per cent of the total population.

17.7%
15.8%
66.5%

0–14 Total 10.7million (Male 5.5m/Female 5.2m)
15–64 Total 40.1million (Male 20.3m/Female19.8m)
65+ Total 9.6million (Male 4.1m/Female 5.5m)

▲
▲ Population by age and sex.

At Speakers' Corner in London, anyone – of any culture, ethnic group, religion or nationality – can speak openly. ▼
▼

Language and age

The official language of Great Britain is English. Around 26 per cent of people in Wales speak Welsh. Scots Gaelic is spoken by about 60,000 people. Ethnic communities often keep alive their native languages by using them when talking in their homes.

The birth rate and death rate are low, as a result of good living standards. Men live to around 76 years of age and women to about 81. Overall, the population is gradually ageing. More than 16 per cent of people are over the age of 65 and this figure will rise to about 20 per cent by 2021.

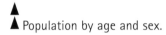

Immigrants granted British citizenship in 2004.

 The south-east is the most heavily populated region. Here, commuters in London wait to get on an urban train.

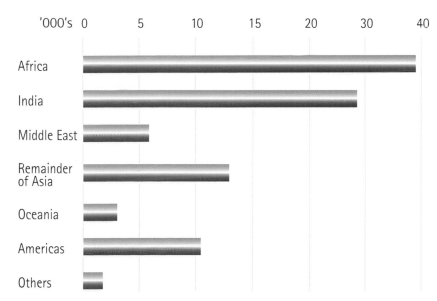

'000's

Africa	
India	
Middle East	
Remainder of Asia	
Oceania	
Americas	
Others	

 Web Search ▶▶

▶ **www.statistics.gov.uk**
Up-to-the-minute facts and figures about Great Britain and the United Kingdom.

▶ **www.ukonline.gov.uk**
▶ **www.wales.gov.uk**
▶ **www.scotlandline.com**
▶ **www.discovernorthern ireland.com**
Information on all parts of Britain and the United Kingdom.

▲ In rural areas, traditional homes range from small cottages and terraces, like these, to large country houses.

Population Density

Because of its relatively small size compared to its population, Great Britain has one of the world's highest population densities.

Population - people per sq mi/km

2,600 or over	1000 or over
1500-2600	600-999
780-1500	300-599
390-780	150-299
under 390	under 150

Edinburgh

Manchester

Birmingham

Cardiff

London

Urban and Rural Life

Almost 250 people live in each square kilometre of Great Britain, more than twice as many as in neighbouring France. Over 90 per cent of British people live in towns and cities.

As cities become more crowded, many people have chosen to live outside and commute into the city. As a result, once-tiny villages have sprawled outwards with new housing estates and shopping areas.

Building new houses and converting old ones

Rows of red-brick terraced houses are a common sight in the industrial cities that thrived in the late-19th and early-20th centuries. Many of these grew up around coalfields, for example in south Wales and in the north-east of England. During the 1950s and 1960s, blocks of council-owned flats were built to fill areas devastated by World War II bombing. By the late-20th century, council tenants were encouraged to buy their properties; the number of owner-occupiers of houses and flats increased from 49 per cent in 1970 to 70 per cent by 2003.

Many large, old family homes, particularly in cities such as London, have been converted into flats for people to buy or rent. In recent years, new housing, offices and shopping complexes have been built in the run-down docklands of major cities, including Liverpool and Edinburgh.

◀◀ Traffic in London, which is the largest city in Great Britain with a population of over 7 million.

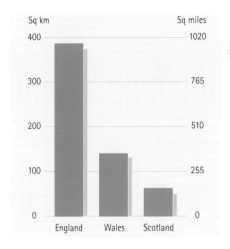

▲▲ Population density.

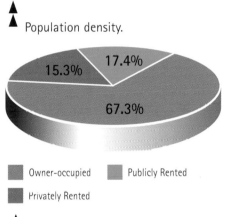

17.4%

15.3%

67.3%

■ Owner-occupied ■ Publicly Rented

■ Privately Rented

▲ Ownership and rental of the 25 million homes in Great Britain.

Web Search ▶▶

▶ **www.streetmap.co.uk**
Find and print a streetmap of any British town or village.

▶ **www.housing.org.uk**
News and the latest housing plans from the National Housing Federation.

11

Farming and Fishing

Freshwater fishing

Today, most inland fishing is done for sport, not a commercial catch. There are, however, salmon and trout farms, particularly in Scotland. Traditional freshwater catches include:

- Salmon
- Trout
- Roach
- Perch
- Freshwater eel
- Pike
- Grayling

A small coastal fishing boat in harbour.

▼

British farming and fishing are highly mechanized, although in Wales and Scotland there are still small farmsteads. Generally, the lowland areas of Britain have rich soil suitable for arable farming. In the hills and mountains, plentiful rainfall keeps the grass green for grazing animals.

The most important crops are cereals (wheat, barley and oats), oilseed rape, sugarbeet and potatoes. Some of these are grown as animal feed. There are fruit farms and market gardens in areas such as Kent, in south-east England.

Sheep and cattle are the most numerous livestock, followed by pigs and poultry. Wales, in particular, is famous for its lamb and mutton. Scotland is noted for Aberdeen Angus, a hardy breed of beef cattle, but most cattle make up dairy herds. Dairy products include milk, butter and a wide range of cheeses, most famously English Cheddar and Stilton.

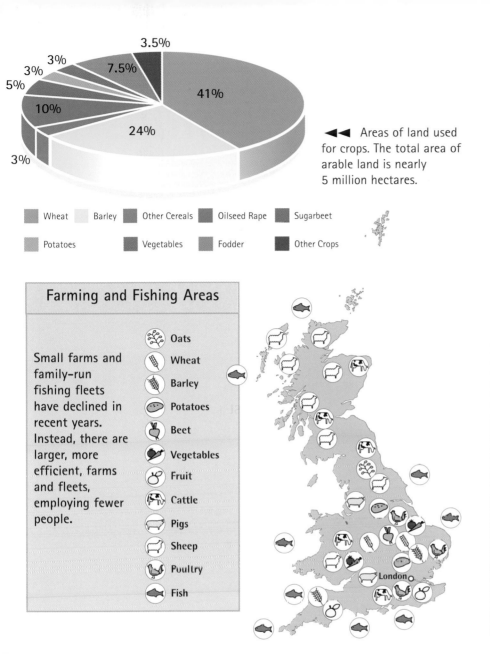

3.5%

3%

3%

5%

7.5%

41%

10%

24%

3%

◀◀ Areas of land used for crops. The total area of arable land is nearly 5 million hectares.

- ◼ Wheat
- ◻ Barley
- ◼ Other Cereals
- ◼ Oilseed Rape
- ◼ Sugarbeet
- ◼ Potatoes
- ◼ Vegetables
- ◼ Fodder
- ◼ Other Crops

Farming and Fishing Areas

Small farms and family-run fishing fleets have declined in recent years. Instead, there are larger, more efficient, farms and fleets, employing fewer people.

- Oats
- Wheat
- Barley
- Potatoes
- Beet
- Vegetables
- Fruit
- Cattle
- Pigs
- Sheep
- Poultry
- Fish

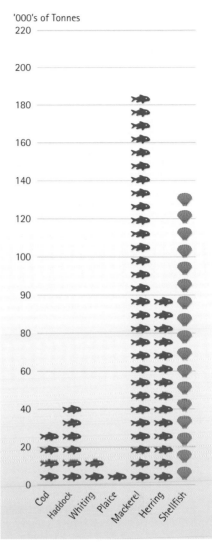

'000's of Tonnes

▲ Fish catches per year made by Great Britain's sea-going boats.

The fishing industry

The British fishing fleet numbers under 7,000 vessels. They land over 600,000 tonnes of seafish a year, more than 65 per cent of the country's needs.

Intensive overfishing has reduced the numbers of fish caught and, when Britain became part of the European Community (EC – now renamed the EU), it agreed not to fish beyond 320 kilometres from its coast. In spite of this, the Dogger Bank in the North Sea remains one of the world's richest fishing grounds. The chief catches are cod, haddock, whiting, mackerel, turbot, herring and plaice.

Web Search ▶▶

▶ www.defra.gov.uk
Details of farming and fishing from the Department for Environment, Food and Rural Affairs.

13

Resources and Industry

Britain is one of the top industrial countries in the world. Although the reserves of iron and coal that fuelled its development have declined, British industry still contributes about 26 per cent of the country's gross domestic product (GDP).

Britain produces 100 million tonnes of coal each year. Most of this is burned in power stations. As a result of the oil and gas reserves discovered in the North Sea during the 1960s, Britain has more energy resources than any other EU country. Britain's mineral resources include tin and zinc, and quarries supply sand, gravel and limestone.

Manufacturing

Electronics, cars and aerospace equipment dominate manufacturing. Factories also make chemicals (especially medicines), man-made fibres, plastics and furniture. Sheffield steel and silver are world-famous. Other industries include food, drinks and tobacco, printing and publishing, and the 'rag trade' (clothing). Overall, manufacturing employs around 19 per cent of the workforce.

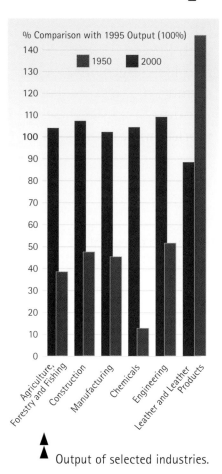

% Comparison with 1995 Output (100%)

■ 1950   ■ 2000

Agriculture, Forestry and Fishing · Construction · Manufacturing · Chemicals · Engineering · Leather and Leather Products

Output of selected industries.

All kinds of services

Service industries include computer support, insurance and management consultancy. These industries have taken over from manufacturing as the major employers, with 80 per cent of all workers. They are also the biggest and fastest-growing, with expansion occuring in shops, restaurants, travel agents, fitness centres and finance. The London Stock Exchange helps make Britain one of the world's major financial centres.

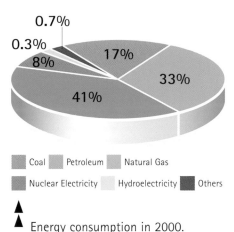

0.7%
0.3%
8%
17%
33%
41%

⬛ Coal ⬛ Petroleum ⬛ Natural Gas
⬛ Nuclear Electricity ⬛ Hydroelectricity ⬛ Others

▲
▲ Energy consumption in 2000.

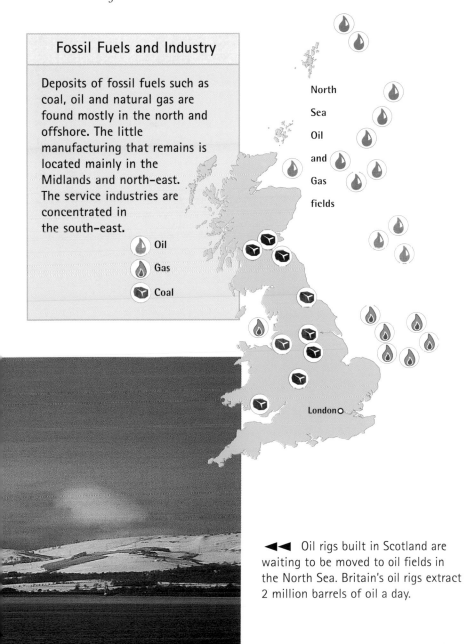

Fossil Fuels and Industry

Deposits of fossil fuels such as coal, oil and natural gas are found mostly in the north and offshore. The little manufacturing that remains is located mainly in the Midlands and north-east. The service industries are concentrated in the south-east.

💧 Oil
💧 Gas
⬛ Coal

North
Sea
Oil
and
Gas
fields

London⃝

◄◄ Oil rigs built in Scotland are waiting to be moved to oil fields in the North Sea. Britain's oil rigs extract 2 million barrels of oil a day.

📎 Major changes

The last 25 years have seen dramatic changes in British energy production and use. Since 1975, output of crude oil has increased 80 times, coal production has more than halved and output of natural gas and nuclear electricity have trebled.

Today, Britain uses only 10 per cent more energy than it did in 1975. However, the output of its industries has doubled. This is because its use of energy is far more efficient. Also, its power stations produce far less pollution than they did in 1975. Britain's anti-pollution measures are among the best in the world.

🌐 Web Search ►►

► **www.dti.gov.uk**
The website of the UK's Department of Trade and Industry.

Transport

R oads and motorways are Britain's primary domestic transport routes. There is also an extensive rail network and several internal air routes.

At the beginning of the 20th century, railway trains and canal barges were the main means of transporting heavy goods. Now, around 62 per cent are carried by lorries. The biggest road-users are car drivers, and about 73 per cent of households have at least one car. New roads have been built to accommodate the extra traffic, but gridlock is still a problem in many places during rush hours.

Some workers commute to work by train, although these services, too, are overstretched. Britain's rail network covers 16,659 kilometres. Various private rail companies operate the trains and a central company called Network Rail maintains the tracks.

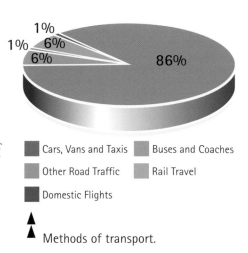

1%
1%
6%
6%
86%

- Cars, Vans and Taxis
- Buses and Coaches
- Other Road Traffic
- Rail Travel
- Domestic Flights

▲ Methods of transport.

Britain has 31.2 million registered road vehicles, travelling on 3,431 kilometres of motorways and 389,500 kilometres of public roads. ▼

Motorway Links

London is the hub of the motorway network. The M25, opened in 1986, is a circular motorway that allows heavy traffic to bypass the city. Motorway links from London to Dover and Folkestone allow vehicles access to ferries and Channel Tunnel trains that connect with continental Europe.

Edinburgh

Manchester

Birmingham

Cardiff   London — M25

— Motorways

Air and sea routes

Air traffic in Britain has increased dramatically in recent years. London has three main airports – Heathrow, Gatwick and Stansted. Together with the airports at Glasgow, Manchester, Prestwick and Aberdeen, these handle about 75 per cent of passenger air traffic.

Shipping is the main form of cargo transport in to and out of Britain, despite the opening of the Channel Tunnel to France in 1994. However, the number of people travelling by sea has declined. Ferries from Dover, the busiest sea port, carry passengers to mainland Europe.

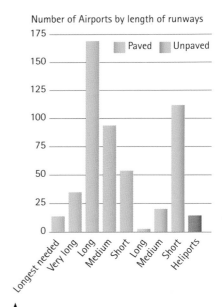

Number of Airports by length of runways

▲ Britain's airports and heliports. Heathrow is Europe's busiest airport; nearly 68 million passengers pass through it each year.

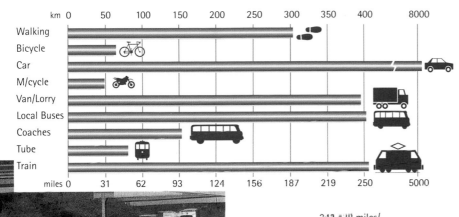

◄◄ Average yearly distances per person by type of travel.

243,438 miles/ 389,500 km

10,796 miles/ 17,274 km

2,000 miles/ 3,200 km

Railtracks   Roads   Canals

▲ Total length of roads, rail and canals.

Web Search ►►

► **www.rail.co.uk**
Britain's railway companies, timetables and travel services.

► **www.highways.gov.uk**
The Highways Agency.

► **www.caa.co.uk**
The Civil Aviation Association.

► **www.abports.co.uk**
The Association of British Ports.

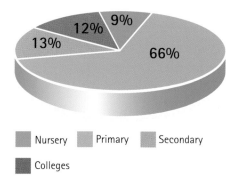

In many secondary schools, children must wear a school uniform.

◄◄ Students relaxing outside King's College, Cambridge University, one of the oldest in Britain. It dates from the 13th century.

9%

12%

13%

66%

Nursery   Primary   Secondary

Colleges

Number of schools at all levels.

Education

British children must attend primary school from the age of 5. At age 11 they attend secondary school until they are 16. Education is free for all children from 5 to 19, but about 6 per cent of children go to private, fee-paying, schools.

Children attend school from Monday to Friday and, in some private schools, on Saturday morning. The school year is up to 39 weeks long, usually divided into three terms. Since 1988 there has been a National Curriculum for England and Wales. This means that all schools teach the same subjects to the same levels of difficulty. Scotland has its own curriculum system, but the subjects and topics taught are much the same.

From school to university

Children under the age of about five do not have to go to school, but may attend nursery from the age of three. Spaces are limited, but there are many private nurseries.

At age five, children begin primary school. Here, they are taught reading, writing and maths skills. They also study art, music, religious education and computing. There are lessons in simple geography, history and science.

Ninety-one per cent of children over 11 go to a mixed-sex comprehensive school. For the first three years they study a range of subjects and begin at least one modern language. At age 14 or 15, they start to study for public exams, called GCSEs in England and Wales, or SSGs in Scotland. Children may then leave school or go to college to study for AS/A2-Level exams, or Highers in Scotland.

Students gain a university place based on their exam results. In England, if students are unable to pay their tuition fees and living expenses themselves, they can get a government loan. Students in Scotland receive a grant.

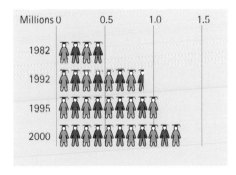

DATABASE

TV Education
The Open University was set up in 1971. Its students are mostly adults who did not go on to higher education straight after school. They follow correspondence courses, allowing them to study and have a job at the same time. BBC television and radio programmes back up the course work.

▲ Growth in the number of university students.

⊕ **Web Search** ▶▶

▶ **www.dfes.gov.uk**
Statistics and other information from Britain's Department for Education and Training.

# Sport and Leisure

▲ Bowls is a traditional British sport. It is played both indoors and outdoors.

Many of the world's most famous sports began in Britain, including cricket, golf, football and rugby. Horse-racing is another important spectator sport. In their leisure time, the British enjoy a range of pastimes, including rambling, cycling, golf and bowls.

To many, football is Britain's national sport, and some of its teams are world famous, among them Manchester United, Arsenal and Liverpool. The domestic season runs from August to May. Regular fans attend matches at grounds around the country, while international games attract huge TV audiences. More than 20 million people in Britain tuned in to watch England play France in the Euro 2004 competition in Portugal.

Rugby originated at Rugby School in Warwickshire. Today, there are two versions of the game: rugby league has 13 players each team and rugby union has 15. The Welsh, in particular, are keen rugby union players and key clubs include Cardiff, Swansea and Neath.

Golf, horse-racing and tennis

Scotland is traditionally regarded as the home of golf and England as the home of tennis. The most important golf club in Scotland, at the seaside town of St Andrews near Dundee, has regularly hosted the British Open Championship since 1873. The world's most famous tennis club, at Wimbledon, in London, hosts a major international tennis tournament each summer.

The key horse-racing events are the Derby, held at Epsom in Surrey, and the Grand National steeplechase held at Aintree, just outside Liverpool. Another equestrian sport is polo, brought to Britain from India in the 19th century by Army officers. One of the most famous polo players is Prince Charles, the heir to the throne of Great Britain.

▲ Football internationals are played at larger stadiums across the country, including the Millennium Stadium in Cardiff. National competitions include English, Scottish and Welsh Football Association (FA) league and knock-out championships.

Members '000's

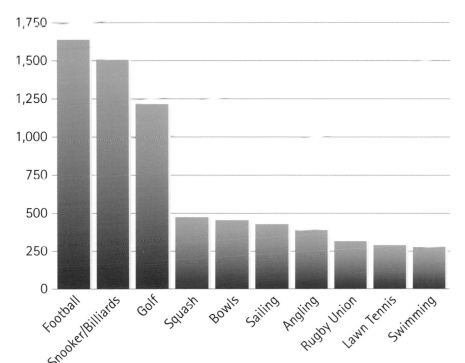

◄◄ Number of people belonging to sports clubs.

🌐 **Web Search** ▶▶

▶ **www.culture.gov.uk**
Government department for Culture, Media and Sport.

▶ **www.sportengland.org**
▶ **www.ssc.org.uk**
▶ **www.sports-council-wales.co.uk**
England's, Scotland's, Northern Ireland's and Wales' sporting bodies.

Daily Life and Religion

In Britain, the usual working and school weeks run from Monday to Friday, with the weekend free for leisure. The working day usually runs from 9.30 a.m. to 5.30 p.m., but many people work flexible hours, night shifts and at weekends.

Television is the main form of relaxation. Adults spend an average of nearly 2.5 hours a day watching TV or listening to the radio. Shopping is a popular weekend pastime. People shop at local markets, large city-centre shopping malls or out-of-town hypermarkets.

People shop at Petticoat Lane street market in London . ▼

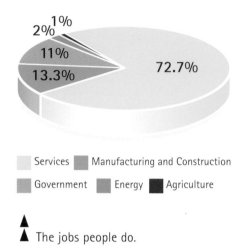

1%
2%
11%
13.3%
72.7%

Services Manufacturing and Construction
Government Energy Agriculture

▲ The jobs people do.

Religion

The official religion of Great Britain is the Anglican Church, or Church of England. Sixty-eight per cent of the population are registered as Anglicans and 22.5 per cent as Roman Catholics. Other Christian groups include Presbyterians (particularly in Scotland), Methodists (particularly in Wales) and Baptists. Britain has the second-largest Jewish community in Europe. There are growing communities of Muslims, Hindus and Sikhs.

Health care

Public healthcare is provided by the National Health Service (NHS), set up by the government in 1948. People can visit their family doctors and also receive free hospital treatment. Dentists and opticians provide free care only for people on low incomes, for children and for old age pensioners. There are also private hospitals and doctors. These are paid for mostly by medical insurance, which some companies provide for the benefit of their employees.

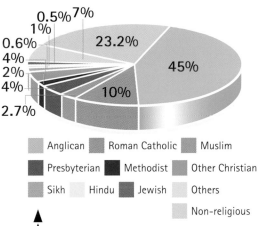

0.5% 7%
1%
0.6%
4%
2%
4%
2.7%
23.2%
45%
10%

Anglican · Roman Catholic · Muslim
Presbyterian · Methodist · Other Christian
Sikh · Hindu · Jewish · Others
Non-religious

▲ Percentages of people registered for different religions. Many Britons do not actively practise their religion.

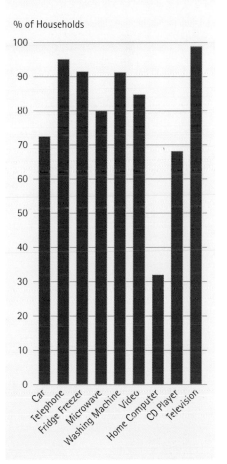

% of Households

Car, Telephone, Fridge Freezer, Microwave, Washing Machine, Video, Home Computer, CD Player, Television

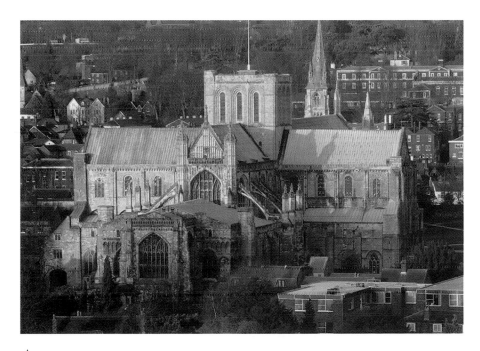

▲ Towns such as Winchester in England are built around an historic cathedral.

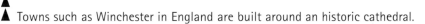

▲ Ownership of appliances in Britain.

Arts and Media

Britain produces world-class newspapers, books and television programmes. Its musicians play on one in five of all recordings made worldwide, and theatres are flourishing. As well as world-famous galleries and museums, Britain has many small art collections.

Millions of people travel to Britain each year, visiting art galleries and theatres. *The Mousetrap*, a play in London's West End, has been staged for over 50 years. It is the world's longest-running theatre production. The Cardiff and the Edinburgh International Festivals are just two of many cultural events that take place all over the country. They are spectacular celebrations of dance, music and literature.

Web Search ►►

► **www.visitbritain.com**
Includes direct links to many of Britain's tourist attractions.

► **www.scotlandonline. com/entertainment**
Features the latest exhibitions, gigs and movie reviews for Scotland.

► **www.resource.gov.uk**
Britain's museum website.

A crowd of tourists and local people watch a street performer at the Edinburgh Festival. ▼

Circulation (2005) in millions

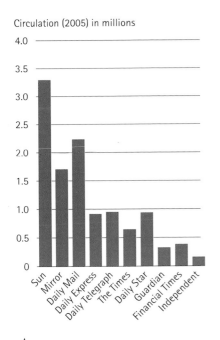

▲ A higher proportion of British people read newspapers than any other nation in the world.

Millions of visitors

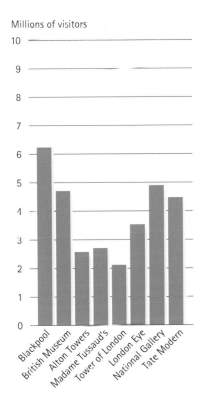

Cinema and literature

The cinema industry in Great Britain is thriving once again. It was world-famous in the 1930s and 1940s. Alfred Hitchcock, one of the greatest film directors of all time, was born in London. Many films have been based on the works of the British writers William Shakespeare and Charles Dickens. Famous poets include Dylan Thomas, William Wordsworth and Robert Burns.

Television and newspapers

The British Broadcasting Corporation (BBC) broadcasts two terrestrial television channels. Its many radio stations include five national ones and the World Service. ITV, Channel 4 and Channel 5 are independent commercial TV channels. There are many commercial radio stations. British viewers can also receive satellite and cable TV programmes from all over the world.

Britain has more than 100 daily newspapers. The most famous are *The Times*, the *Mirror*, the *Sun* and the *Guardian*. The biggest-selling regional paper is the Scottish *Glasgow Daily Record* (circulation 714,636). There are hundreds of magazines for both adults and children.

◄◄ Millions of people visit Britain's museums, castles, theme parks and stately homes. Most foreign tourists come from the USA, Europe and Japan.

Government

The King or Queen is officially the head of state of Great Britain, but the nation is actually governed by Parliament. Laws are made in Parliament but have to be approved by the monarch. Members of Parliament (MPs) are elected by the British people.

Parliamentary elections are held once every five years, or less. Everyone aged 18 or over may vote in a general election. The country is divided into groups of around 90,000 voters, each electing one Member of Parliament, who will sit in the House of Commons in London.

There are 659 MPs in total, and most belong to the Labour Party, Conservative Party or Liberal Democratic Party. The party that has most MPs after an election forms a Government led by a Cabinet of between 10 and 30 senior MPs and the Prime Minister, the leader of the party.

Regional government and Europe

There are also a Scottish parliament and Welsh and Northern Ireland assemblies. These bodies take decisions about the running of Scotland, Wales and Northern Ireland. Local government departments deal with each region or county. Aspects of government such as agriculture and employment are increasingly being controlled not by Britain but by the European Parliament, to which British people elect MEPs (Members of the European Parliament) to represent them.

The clock tower of the Houses of Parliament. It is often referred to as Big Ben, but this is actually the name of the bell inside the tower. A light shines at the top of the tower when Parliament is in session late in the evening. ▼

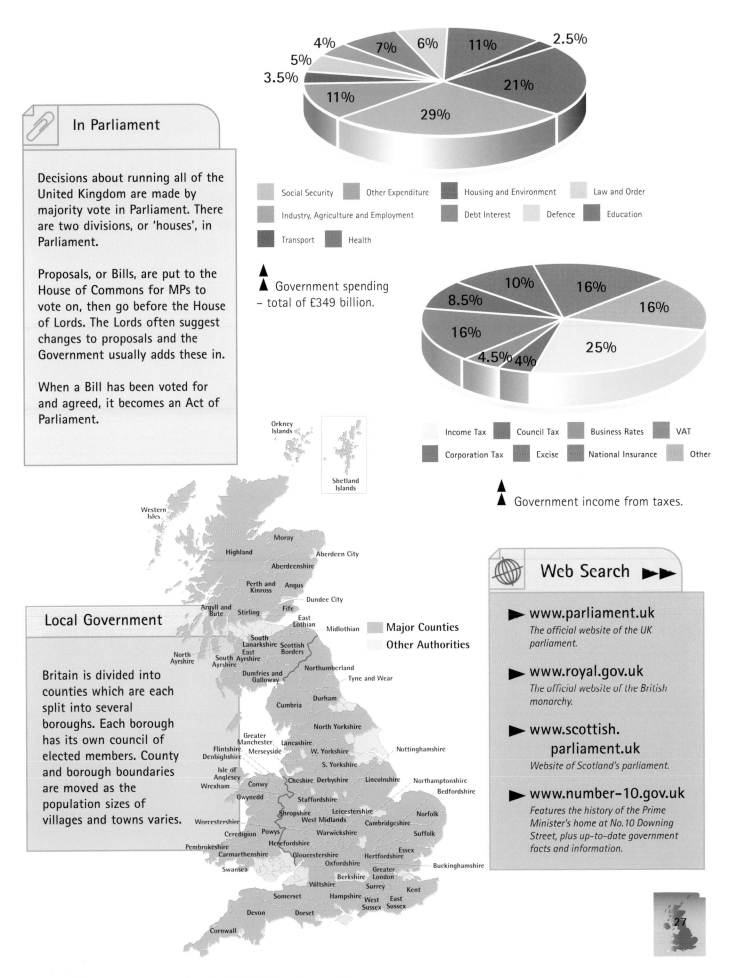

In Parliament

Decisions about running all of the United Kingdom are made by majority vote in Parliament. There are two divisions, or 'houses', in Parliament.

Proposals, or Bills, are put to the House of Commons for MPs to vote on, then go before the House of Lords. The Lords often suggest changes to proposals and the Government usually adds these in.

When a Bill has been voted for and agreed, it becomes an Act of Parliament.

Government spending pie chart: 4%, 5%, 3.5%, 11%, 7%, 6%, 11%, 2.5%, 21%, 29%

Social Security · Other Expenditure · Housing and Environment · Law and Order · Industry, Agriculture and Employment · Debt Interest · Defence · Education · Transport · Health

▲▲ Government spending – total of £349 billion.

Government income pie chart: 10%, 16%, 8.5%, 16%, 16%, 4.5%, 4%, 25%

Income Tax · Council Tax · Business Rates · VAT · Corporation Tax · Excise · National Insurance · Other

▲▲ Government income from taxes.

Local Government

Britain is divided into counties which are each split into several boroughs. Each borough has its own council of elected members. County and borough boundaries are moved as the population sizes of villages and towns varies.

Map labels:
Orkney Islands, Shetland Islands, Western Isles, Moray, Highland, Aberdeen City, Aberdeenshire, Perth and Kinross, Angus, Dundee City, Argyll and Bute, Stirling, Fife, East Lothian, Midlothian, South Lanarkshire, Scottish Borders, North Ayrshire, East Ayrshire, South Ayrshire, Dumfries and Galloway, Northumberland, Tyne and Wear, Durham, Cumbria, North Yorkshire, Greater Manchester, Lancashire, W. Yorkshire, Nottinghamshire, Flintshire, Merseyside, Denbighshire, S. Yorkshire, Isle of Anglesey, Cheshire, Derbyshire, Lincolnshire, Northamptonshire, Wrexham, Conwy, Bedfordshire, Gwynedd, Staffordshire, Shropshire, Leicestershire, Norfolk, West Midlands, Cambridgeshire, Worcestershire, Warwickshire, Suffolk, Ceredigion, Powys, Herefordshire, Essex, Pembrokeshire, Gloucestershire, Hertfordshire, Carmarthenshire, Oxfordshire, Greater London, Buckinghamshire, Swansea, Berkshire, Wiltshire, Surrey, Kent, Somerset, Hampshire, West Sussex, East Sussex, Devon, Dorset, Cornwall

Major Counties · Other Authorities

Web Search ►►

► **www.parliament.uk**
The official website of the UK parliament.

► **www.royal.gov.uk**
The official website of the British monarchy.

► **www.scottish.parliament.uk**
Website of Scotland's parliament.

► **www.number-10.gov.uk**
Features the history of the Prime Minister's home at No.10 Downing Street, plus up-to-date government facts and information.

Place in the World

In 1900, Great Britain was the centre of the British Empire, a group of colonies all over the world. By 1970, Britain had granted independence to most of its territories abroad and its influence weakened. Despite this, Great Britain retains a role in world politics.

Britain's empire did not simply disappear. In 1931 it became the Commonwealth, an association of countries around the world formerly ruled by Britain, including Australia, India, Canada, Nigeria and Jamaica.

Britain has a permanent seat on the Security Council of the United Nations (UN). Along with the United States and the Soviet Union, Britain led the way in founding this organization at the end of World War II. The UN's purpose is to maintain world security and it has peace-keeping forces in many troubled parts of the world.

Members of the British Royal Family in 2000, including Queen Elizabeth II and the Queen Mother (centre) and Prince Charles (second from right). All members act as ambassadors for Britain overseas. The Queen is head of the Commonwealth. ▼

▲ Oxfam, a British aid relief organization, works with NATO forces in Kosovo.

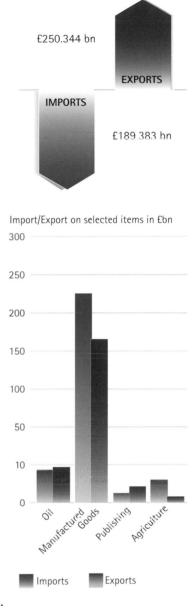

£250.344 bn

EXPORTS

IMPORTS

£189.383 bn

Import/Export on selected items in £bn

Imports   Exports

▲ Imports and exports – selected major categories.

NATO and the EU

Britain was also a founder member of the North Atlantic Treaty Organization (NATO), a military alliance between the United States and several European countries that has existed since 1949.

Britain joined the European Economic Community (later renamed the European Community) in 1973. Today, an overall community of western European nations known as the European Union (EU) works towards greater co-operation between all the member countries. It allows free movement of tourists, exchange of students and workers, and encourages trade between members. The EU also promotes care of the environment.

Although half of Britain's trade is with other EU countries, the United States remains Britain's single biggest trading partner. Many British people think of themselves as separate and different from continental Europeans.

Web Search ▶▶

▶ www.nationalarchives.gov.uk

Website of the National Archives, which holds government documents from AD 1066 to the present-day.

Area:
229,991 sq km

Population size:
60,441,457

Capital city:
London (population 7,421,209)

Longest river:
Severn (354 km)

Highest mountain:
Ben Nevis (1,343 m)

Largest lake:
Loch Lomond (71 sq km)

Flag:
The countries that make up Britain each have their own flag. England's is a red cross on a white background and Scotland's a diagonal white cross on a blue background. The Welsh flag features a red dragon on a green and white background. The UK's national flag is the Union Jack, which combines the crosses of St George of England (red on white), St Andrew of Scotland (diagonal white on blue) and St Patrick of Ireland (diagonal red on white).

▲ Stonehenge, a prehistoric circle of stones on Salisbury Plain, southern England.

Official language:
English

Currency:
Pound sterling (£)

Major resources:
Oil, gas, coal, tin, limestone, iron ore, salt, clay, chalk, gypsum, lead, silica

Major exports:
Manufactured goods, machinery, fuels, chemicals, transport equipment, financial services

National holidays and major events:
New Year's Day (1 January),
Holocaust Day (27 January),
St David's Day (1 March),
Oxford v. Cambridge University
 Boat Race (last week in March),
Good Friday, Easter Sunday and
 Easter Monday (March or April),
Grand National horse-race (first
 Saturday in April),

St George's Day (23 April),
Early May Bank Holiday
 (first Monday in May),
Spring Bank Holiday
 (last Monday in May),
Queen's official birthday (June),
Royal Ascot (mid June),
Royal National Eisteddfod of Wales
 (early August),
Edinburgh Festival (August),
Summer Bank Holiday (August),
Notting Hill Carnival
 (last weekend in August),
Highland Games (early September),
Guy Fawkes' Day (5 November),
Remembrance Day (Sunday nearest
 11 November),
St Andrew's Day (30 November),
Christmas Day (25 December),
Boxing Day (26 December),
New Year's Eve/Hogmanay
 (31 December)

Religions:
Anglican, Roman Catholic, Muslim, Presbyterian, Methodist, Sikh, Hindu, Jewish

Glossary

AGRICULTURE
Farming.

ARABLE
Land used for growing crops rather than raising livestock.

BIRTH RATE
The number of live births in one year per 1,000 women of childbearing age.

CLIMATE
The range of weather in a region over time.

COMMUTE
Repeatedly making the same journey from one particular place to another.

CURRICULUM
A programme of study.

DEATH RATE
The number of deaths in a year per 1,000 of the population.

ECONOMY
The organization of a country's money and resources.

EMPIRE
A group of colonies ruled by a single country.

ETHNIC
Belonging to a particular race or culture.

EXPORTS
Goods sold to a foreign country.

FERTILE
Land suitable for growing crops.

GOVERNMENT
The organization that sets and enforces laws for one nation.

GROSS DOMESTIC PRODUCT (GDP)
The total value of all the goods and services produced by a country in a year.

IMPORTS
Goods bought from a foreign country.

MANUFACTURING
Using machinery to make products from raw materials.

MONARCH
A hereditary head of state.

NATIONAL ASSEMBLY
An assembly of elected representatives that governs a country.

NATIVE
Belonging naturally to a place.

PARLIAMENT
A seat of government. The UK parliament is divided into the House of Commons and the House of Lords.

POLLUTION
Damage to the environment.

POPULATION DENSITY
The average number of people living on a particular area of land.

PRINCIPALITY
A territory controlled by a prince, in the same way that a kingdom is controlled by a king or queen.

PROVINCE
A part of a country or state that has a particular identity.

QUARRY
A site where natural material, such as rock, is extracted from the ground.

RESOURCES
A country's supplies of energy, natural materials and minerals.

RURAL
Relating to the countryside.

SUBJECT
(1) An area of study, for example at school; (2) a person ruled over by a monarch.

URBAN
Relating to towns and cities.

Index